OLD-WORLD

A play in two parts by
ALEKSEI ARBUZOV

Translated by
ARIADNE NICOLAEFF

SAMUEL FRENCH

LONDON
NEW YORK TORONTO SYDNEY HOLLYWOOD

FOR AMATEUR PRODUCTION ENQUIRIES

UNITED KINGDOM AND WORLD
EXCLUDING NORTH AMERICA
plays@samuelfrench.co.uk
020 7255 4302/01

Each title is subject to availability from Samuel French, depending upon country of performance.

OLD-WORLD

The British première was presented by the Royal Shakespeare Company at the Aldwych Theatre, London on 12th October 1976, with the following cast:

Lidya Vasilyevna—she is not quite sixty	Peggy Ashcroft
Rodion Nikolayevich—he is sixty-five	Anthony Quayle

Directed by Terry Hands
Designer Ralph Koltai
Music composed by Ian Kellam

The action takes place in August 1968 on the Riga Coast

The song by Bella Akhmadulina, translated by Ariadne Nicolaeff. Enquiries regarding the music for the song should be addressed to Samuel French Ltd.

TRANSLATOR'S NOTE

Old-World is a fairly free translation of *Staramodnaya Komediya* by Aleksei Arbuzov. It contains alterations made during rehearsals without reference to the Russian text. I was invited to attend at the run-through stage just before Aleksei Arbuzov came to London. He asked for some of the cuts to be put back. And I have now put back some passages which were over-simplified and weakened the play in the Aldwych production. I have also added a couple of new lines Aleksei Arbuzov wrote at the director's request which were not used. Otherwise this is the version at the Aldwych Theatre. Even if I wanted to, at this stage I could not possibly disentangle the dialogue from the intonations of Dame Peggy Ashcroft and Anthony Quayle. They both gave superb performances. Dame Peggy received the Society of West End Theatre's 1976 Award for Actress of the Year in a New Play.

Ariadne Nicolaeff

PART ONE

SCENE ONE

Her sixth day.

I remember this started at the end of July in 1968 on the shore of the Gulf of Riga.

That bright sunny day Rodion Nikolayevich, medical head of the sanatorium, who looked striking and very respectable, sat in a wicker chair with his legs crossed. He was not particularly fond of staying in his consulting room out of surgery hours. There was plenty of time for that when it rained. On sunny days tearing himself away from his work, he enjoyed looking up at the blue sky and the shrubs and trees around him. He had installed some plain garden furniture in the shade of a large chestnut tree by the windows of his consulting room, thus adding a summer extension to his office.

That memorable morning Rodion Nikolayevich was glancing through some papers, when Lidya Vasilyevna appeared before him for the first time. I regret I cannot describe her as young. But does age matter when you look at a woman and realize how fascinating she had been in her youth? Taking a good look, you also realize that life had not always smiled at her and now hardly at all. All the same, that day when she first appeared before Rodion Nikolayevich her dress was not without elegance. I repeat, not without elegance, though rather loud. On seeing him she observed him closely and addressed him rather haughtily.

She   I rather think, yes, I am quite sure, you're Rodion Nikolayevich.

He   That's right.

She   Then you must be the medical head of this sanatorium.

He   Right again.

She   I don't understand why you're smiling.

He   Oddly enough, neither do I.

She   You're still smiling.

He   *(frowns and assumes a solemn mien)* There, you see, I've stopped now.

She   You weren't in your office. On the advice of Velta Radzika, the nurse on duty, I came down into the garden. I'm very glad I spotted you.

He   I'm sorry but out of surgery hours I prefer to be in the garden outside my office windows. Please sit down.

She   Thank you. *(Sits)* Though you might have thought of it earlier.

He   Quite right. Only it didn't occur to me.

She   Why not?

He   Well, I was very surprised when I saw you.

She   *(cold)* What is so surprising about me?

He   I don't know. But I was most surprised. I thought we'd met before.

She   *(just as stern)* Is that what made you laugh?

He   I suppose so.

        Pause.

She   Well, why don't you say something?

He   Should I?

She   Certainly. You asked me to come and have a talk with you.

He   I beg your pardon. Are you staying in our sanatorium?

She   *(proud)* I thought you knew.

He   What is your name?

She   Zherber.

He   Zherber?

She   Lidya Vasilyevna Zherber.

He   Oh, that one?

She   *(with dignity)* That one? What do you mean? What a peculiar expression. *(Sniffs)* That one!

He   I apologize, but you had an appointment at ten o'clock this morning. It's now past one.

She   What nonsense! What does it matter? Now that I am here.

He   *(cautious)* I'm glad you are. But why weren't you here at ten?

She   It's an awkward time. At ten I feed the seagulls. *(Stern)* I feed them every day after breakfast.

He   I think for once you might have fed them a bit later.

She   *(flat statement)* No, it would upset the routine.

He   Is that part of your treatment?

She   Certainly not. I'm independent in everything I do. *(Pause)* What's the name of that tree?

He   *(surprised)* Chestnut.

She   And the shrub?

He   *(even more surprised)* Acacia.

She   It's very important I remember that. It's sad but the last few years I've been madly cut off from nature. I mix up the names of flowers and birds. I just cannot remember who's who. Now I must try and remember it all. *(Pause)* Why don't you say something? Here I am, sitting here with you, wasting my time, but you don't say anything.

You've gone into hiding! Is my cardiogram bad? Or my blood condition poor? Is there something else unpleasant? Don't hide.

He   *(hurriedly)* No, no . . . So far I have no data that need trouble you. It's an entirely different matter. You see . . . Our sanatorium is a medical institution. Not a hotel, not even a convalescent home. We must insist on absolute quiet and order. And yet . . .

She   I'm listening with great interest.

He   Your behaviour has given rise to many complaints. You've only been here six days but the unfavourable comments are piling up. We've never had such an unusual patient, you know.

She   First, I must point out, the word "patient" simply won't do. It's a label. It's bound to depress any normal person who comes here with a clear conscience and an open mind.

He   Well, it's none of my doing. Those are the regulations.

She   *(contemptuous)* "Regulations!" Regulations are made by people who have nothing better to do.

He   Excuse me, if you don't mind . . .

She   What am I accused of?

He   In the first place you prevent everyone from sleeping.

She   *(in icy tones)* In what way do I prevent them from sleeping?

He   In the middle of the night when everyone's in bed, suddenly and unexpectedly you begin reciting poetry out loud.

She   I don't believe it! They don't like poetry! Surely they don't prefer snoring? Do you know, the woman next to me—we'll call her X—snores with such overwhelming power that the flowers on my bedside table wave this way and that—I assure you—they wave with her snoring. At the same time the woman on my other side—we'll call her Y—moans and groans in her sleep so that God only knows what to think about her . . . But you see, I'm quite happy, I don't complain.

He   That's good. But I also have a report here that at first light you suddenly burst into song and wake everyone up.

She   But how can I stop myself on a sunny, summer morning? I don't sing when it rains, you know, I haven't the slightest urge. And I sing very quietly, it's barely audible. *(Sings very quietly)*
>In many countries I have been,
> My squirrel and I . . .

There, would that wake you up?

He   You sing very nicely. But you must understand that some people are very light sleepers. And we mustn't be selfish and deprive them of their early morning sleep.

She   Yes, all right, but why shouldn't they do with a few hours less sleep? After all nothing shortens one's life like the sleep from which you don't wake up. You can miss masses of interesting things. Don't you agree that, on the whole, life in this world is quite interesting?

He   Perfectly true, but early morning sleep . . .

She   *(interrupting)* Do you know, there are some people who've been here for a long time but they've never seen the sunrise. Not once, you know! And the sunrise on the sea is something quite extra-ordinary.

He   Yes, I agree. But there's another thing—according to witnesses, you climb into the garden at night out of the window and return the same way later. Why? People lie awake waiting patiently for your return before they can go to sleep again. But sometimes you stay away for an hour and a half, that's traumatic for them.

She   But, Velta Radzika, the nurse on duty, locks us in for the night. Sometimes I have an overwhelming urge to be in the garden, to enjoy the moonlight, to go to the beach, to be alone with nature . . . You must realize that I'm a townswoman. For years I haven't seen the sea or wandered in the forest . . . Everything all round me here drives me definitely off my head. *(She's suddenly ashamed of her confession)* But I suppose all this leaves you quite cold. For the last half hour you've been taking sweets out of that little box, drugging yourself into a state of oblivion. Please go on sucking them. I sup-pose it's the only thing you're capable of.

He   *(utterly humiliated)* If you don't mind . . .

She   And there is one thing I can say in my defence—I climb through the window very carefully. With great caution.

He   *(reading)* "Leaving by the window last night she knocked over three bottles all of which broke at the same time, waking up everyone in her own ward and the whole of the lower wing."

She   In future, I promise to climb through the window with the utmost caution.

He   Damnation! You really are very difficult to talk to.

She   *(with sympathy)* So I've often been told. I don't know why. When I meet people, my intentions are of the best, as a rule.

He   Now, stop it! You have an extraordinary talent of reducing every-thing to nothing.

She   Naturally, I try and keep up with the times. Have you anything else against me, Doctor?

He   As an experiment, so that we may get to know our . . . hm . . . patients, on their arrival we ask them to fill in this form. Frankly I was utterly puzzled by your replies. In the first place against the question of your age you simply put a dash.

She   *(stiffly)* I think it's tactless to ask a woman her age. The age of all Soviet citizens is a purely personal matter. Why this unhealthy curiosity? I haven't asked you how old you are.

He   There's nothing to prevent you. Unlike you with your obscure feminine reasoning, I say quite openly I'm nearly sixty-five.

She   You don't mean it?

He   Mean what?

She   I thought you were much younger.

He   Hm . . . Did you? Well, anyway that is my age.

She   Never mind, I like your honesty, and I'll try and respond with equal frankness. I'm not quite sixty. Does that satisfy you?

He   I really don't know why it should satisfy me. *(Writes)* "Fifty-nine." Now, let's go on to the question of your profession. Why was your reply so vague? "I work in the circus."

She   But I do work in the circus.

He   Doing what? What is your profession?

She   Is that going to cure my arteriosclerosis? Diagnosed at long last by your doctors, though really I haven't got it.

He   Your profession, woman! What do you do in the circus? Do you turn somersaults? Play the drum? Swallow live frogs?

She   I do conjuring tricks. What else can a woman do at my age? Conjuring tricks. I hope we've finished with that question.

He   "Conjuring tricks." Why haven't you filled in the space about your family? *(Pause)* Are you married?

She   Sometimes that question is too complicated to answer simply.

He   Damn it, are you or aren't you married?

She   *(after pause)* You know, it's nice of you to get so worked up. I'm rather touched. No, I am not married. Definitely not. Now are you satisfied? Have you any more questions? No? Then I shall hide nothing and I will tell you that you bore me to distraction. In the whole wide world no one has ever bored me as you have. You ask tactless questions, you try and find out if I'm married or, thank God, not! And you haven't even taken the trouble to put on a white coat! If you ask questions, you should wear a white coat, not that badly pressed jacket with a missing button! It's too awful—you summon me to a serious talk and you munch sweets non-stop. There's a Soviet doctor for you! The shame, the disgrace! I never want to see you again.

He   *(exploding)* Now that's enough! If you must know, I suck sweets non-stop in order to rid myself of the harmful habit of smoking. You're an absurd creature, that's all you are. I'm a very busy man and I haven't time to stand here being made a complete fool of by you. There's another form. Fill it in or leave the sanatorium.

She   *(with dignity)* If you don't behave yourself, I'll send for the police. *(Takes a sweet from his box, pops it into her mouth, bangs the lid of the box shut and goes out slowly)*

He   *(looks after her in astonishment)* What an extraordinary woman!

SCENE TWO

Her eighth day.

A small café on the sea-shore towards evening. It's still marvellous weather.

Lidya Vasilyevna goes to the table where Rodion Niko-layevich is sitting alone having coffee and cake. She carries a glass of tea with lemon and a piece of shortbread on a saucer.

She   *(sitting down at his table)* It's me. I'm delighted to see you here. It's really very nice of you.

He   *(amazed)* Nice? What is?

She   Nice you're here. I adore new friends. I like them so much better than old ones. Old friends always go on and on about something one already knows. But it is just possible new friends might say something new. We only met the day before yesterday. We had such a splendid conversation. I've been thinking of you ever since. *(Pause)* Why are you staring at me pop-eyed?

He   *(utterly confused)* Pop-eyed?

She   Pop-eyed. Certainly.

He   Mm—yes . . . Well, you do appear to be a little inconsistent.

She   So I've often been told. But does it matter? Aren't you delighted with the sun when it appears from behind a cloud? Today I love everyone. Definitely! You too. *(He coughs)* What's the matter?

He   I think something went down the wrong way.

She   You have a sweet tooth. Do you come here often?

He   Sometimes. *(Confidentially)* Their poppy-seed cakes are quite delicious. *(Puts a sweet in his mouth)*

She   By the way, when did you stop smoking?

He   About fifteen years ago.

She   Perhaps you should start smoking again to rid yourself of the harmful habit of sucking sweets?

He   You're right, there are so many problems without a solution.

She   Yes, yes, take today, I mean, right now. I came past this patisserie and I saw you sitting here alone with a piece of cake. I was overwhelmed by a wave of pity.

He   Pity?

She   A thought suddenly struck me—has this man suffered disaster, that on a marvellous day like this he sits alone in the corner of a café drinking his black-black coffee.

He   I think you exaggerate. Really things aren't that bad.

She   Splendid! Can I get you another poppy-seed cake? Today I want
       to have happy faces round me.
He   No, spare me, I've had enough.
She   The point is I've just had a letter from my husband. I gather he's by
       the Caspian Sea. And he wrote and told me something really
       amusing. Apparently, they've had a glut of fish . . .
He   Excuse me but the day before yesterday you said you weren't
       married.
She   Did I?
He   I assure you.
She   And you remembered it! That's very strange. I expect I was angry
       with him. So I said he didn't exist. I do it quite often. It's part of my
       inconsistency which you noticed. In spite of it, my husband loves
       me dearly. So far. He often sends me amusing little presents. He's a
       splendid man. You don't seem at all pleased.
He   Why not? I am pleased. *(Loses his temper for some reason)* I'm
       quite enthralled.
She   Well, one doesn't often meet splendid men nowadays. They're all
       so approximate. Neither one thing nor the other! You look at them
       and you think—how can you be so plain, dim and dull, poor darling.
He   I can't say that I find the women today particularly inspiring either.
She   Not at all?
He   No, I'm afraid not. As the medical head of the sanatorium here, I
       meet thousands of new faces. And some of the ladies that turn up!
       There was one last month—she took off her scarf and her hair was
       pink.
She   Not possible!
He   Yes, pink, bright pink. I'm used to blue hair, mauve hair. We've had
       half a dozen of those. But pink! And then the skirts they wear: these
       minis, maxis, midis! And trousers like a clown—that wide. It's dis-
       graceful! In the twenties young women used to wear little leather
       jackets. They were so becoming. Really quite lovely.
She   Little leather jackets are still worn. Very elegant.
He   But not the same. They're different. Quite different! Not like they
       used to be.
She   But a woman should always keep up with the fashion. She must
       shine, she must be gorgeous! And she must never, never give up.
He   *(stays angry)* That's a dubious statement. Highly dubious. I'll tell
       you what makes a woman attractive: modesty, loyalty, a sense of
       proportion. Nothing to do with all these curls and trinkets. *(Growing
       more heated)* Now take that extraordinary contraption you've got on
       your head. What on earth is it? It might get by on a young girl. But
       you're far from young. You're a mature woman. And that thing—
       I'm sorry I don't know what it is.
She   *(crushed)* You don't know what it is?
He   I'm afraid not.

She   That's sad. I thought . . . I liked this turban so much. *(With hope)* It is a turban, you know.

He   Turban? Is that what you call it? I'd have said it was a hat—a rather ghastly hat that fancies itself.

She   Fancies itself?

He   Why do you wear it? To what purpose? To shine? To attract? Come, Comrade Zherber, it's time you thought of your soul!

She   What utter nonsense! What on earth has my soul got to do with it? My dear man, a real woman must remain seductive to her dying day. Even at death's door!

He   Where have we got to now! Death's door! Who wants a pretty woman in her coffin? You're talking rubbish.

She   You brute! You go too far—why talk of coffins? You ought to be ashamed of yourself. And you even called me an old woman!

He   I did not call you an old woman.

She   You did.

He   I didn't. It's not true.

She   What isn't?

He   You are not an old woman.

She   What am I? A young woman? Another blatant lie!

He   *(losing patience)* No, I see we shall never come to an agreement . . .

She   How interesting. And what is there to come to an agreement about? What's the agenda? *(Really indignant)* So he doesn't like my turban! Take a look at yourself—your button is still missing! And there's another hanging by a thread. I'm simply curious, does your wife never look at you?

He   *(cold)* I'm sorry, Comrade Zherber, but I'm not married.

She   *(the slightest of pauses)* Aren't you?

He   No.

She   All the more reason for keeping yourself tidy. You must have women friends who admire you, who feel for you, even worship you.

He   *(controlling his anger)* Let me tell you, once and for all, I have a job to do and I'm not interested in women. As I've already said, they leave me absolutely cold. The lot! Without exception!

She   I don't believe you! Why tell me these lies? A doctor at a health-resort. And not married, please note. Obviously, you've had no end of affairs.

He   Affairs? Me?

She   Yes, You're quite presentable. Rather striking, I'd say.

He   Striking? Oh, please, don't!

She   Why are you so horrified? Love is natural to a human being, especially to a man.

He   Why are you so cynical?

She   What do you mean? *(Sincere)* I'm talking about love. *(With an irresistible smile)* The play of passion.

He   This is awful!

She   I don't understand?

He   Your whole frivolous attitude! There are certain things one should never joke about. Love is sacred. I do know something about it. I was married once.

She   And you've never loved anyone since?

He   I have loved only her.

She   *(in a whisper)* Incredible.

He   I'm going. I'm sorry but there's nothing I find more unattractive in a woman than cheap cynicism. Your spiritual licence appals me! *(He goes towards the exit)*

She   How will you manage without your sweets?

        He stops.

        (crushed) There they are, on the table where you left them.

He   *(goes back, puts the box in his pocket)* Comrade Zherber, however hard we try, we shall never speak the same language. So in future when we have to meet, I'd prefer to keep our conversation strictly within the bounds of the doctor-patient relationship. Without exception. *(He goes)*

She   *(looks after him)* What an extraordinary man.

        SCENE THREE

        Her eleventh day.

        Riga. Outside Domsky Cathedral. It is late evening and it has just been raining. The sound of organ music from the cathedral is just audible in the distance.

        Lidya Vasilyevna comes out of the cathedral and stops. She looks up at the sky; she may be listening to the music.

        Rodion Nikolayevich appears behind her. As he comes out of the cathedral he sees her standing there alone and approaches her with hesitation.

He   Good evening.

She   *(with indifference)* Oh, it's you?

He   Yes.

She   *(after slight pause)* Were you at the concert?

He   I was sitting quite near you in the twelfth row.

She   I never noticed.

He   No, of course not. You were listening.

She   Yes . . .

He   Why did you leave?

She   *(thinks)* It was enough.

He   What?

She   All that . . . Everything.

He   You have tears in your eyes.

She   I'm not crying. *(Takes out a handkerchief and quickly wipes her eyes)* Why are you so kind today?

He   I wouldn't know.

She   I do. *(Smiles)* It's the music. *(Slight pause)* But why did you leave the concert?

He   I noticed you had no raincoat, no umbrella.

She   What of it?

He   You could get wet.

She   It's stopped raining.

He   It could start again.

She   *(suddenly looks at him closely)* You think ahead. *(With a touch of disapproval)* You shouldn't think ahead when you listen to music.

He   *(slight pause)* Do you like organ music?

She   I don't know. I haven't thought. I haven't heard any for twenty years, perhaps more. Life goes by in such a strange way. Doesn't it? No, it's we who go by. There are so many riches all around us, if we turn and look. But we go by. It's very strange, isn't it? There we were at a concert at Domsky Cathedral. I only came because I thought I ought to. And then he began to play. Suddenly I thought I saw myself, my childhood, Whitsun, our garden in the rain, Christmas, a snow field. Suddenly my memory came back.

He   I often come here. Only a rouble—and it can make you happy. Not everyone, more's the pity.

She   Don't be so superior. Please don't.

He   It's raining again.

She   Only a few drops.

He   Shall I open my umbrella?

She   Let's wait a bit.

> *They walk through the square and the music recedes. They find themselves in an area of narrow streets.*

He   Old Riga by night . . . Amusing, isn't it?

She   I've been here before. I don't like leaving the sea but I'm drawn here to the old town. I love wandering about here when it gets dark. *(Very quietly)* I keep expecting an alchemist from the Middle Ages in a pointed hat to emerge from that narrow door.

He   You're a fantasist.

She   No, I'm a cashier.

He   A cashier?

She   Yes.

He   But you wrote: "I work in the circus."

She   I do. But as a cashier. Not a conjurer. We've been listening to such marvellous music, I can't tell you a lie after that . . . *(Pause)* Do you mind my being a cashier?

He   *(suddenly embarrassed)* No, no, of course not. Why should I?

She   Of course, working in the ring is different. It's quite a different matter. Though the box-office also has its moments. Quite often I have to perform conjuring tricks there. I like my work on the whole. And selling tickets can be incredibly satisfying. We have a very special audience, you know—children, visitors to Moscow and very curious residents. And everyone's pleased if they get a ticket on the day. It isn't like the theatre—our audience knows it's going to enjoy itself. You see, we have very, very brilliant clowns. People, who know, say that our clowns are the best in the world.

He   Really? I'm sorry I'm quite out of touch with clowns. I'm quite cut off in fact!

She   Well, when you come to Moscow, I'll see you get a ticket. Two tickets, if you like.

He   Thank you very much. I really should have a look at the clowns.

She   I have quite an amusing time, you know. Life in the circus is never boring! Everyone is so alive. Social life bubbles like a mountain spring. And I have lots of professional commitments. Some are very engrossing. I never have a free moment. And it's great fun. *(Slight pause)* Only sometimes I come home and there's no one there, it's empty. Well, that's not fun.

He   But your husband?

She   *(not immediately)* He's away.

He   But he'll be coming back, won't he?

She   Some time. He's a very great artiste. And very much in demand. And he's a very, very nice person.

He   So you said.

She   Did I? I'm not surprised. One likes to share the good things. *(Pause)* Have you lived long in these parts?

He   Over twenty years. Ever since the war.

She   Where do you come from?

He   I'm from Leningrad.

She   A wonderful city. I always enjoyed going there. And I never wanted to leave.

He   Yes, there was a time . . . *(Slight pause)* Not the same now.

She   Do you always live alone?

He   No, of course not! My daughter comes to visit me. Quite often, on
        the whole. *(Brightening up)* As a matter of fact she's coming soon.
        I had a telegram. She has her own room in my house. It's semi-
        detached but it's in the country. And I have my own garden. I grow
        strawberries and flowers. I'm a very keen gardener. *(With some
        excitement)* You know, from my daughter's room you can see the
        sea. Sometimes I go up there at night and I sit by the window and
        listen to the sound the sea makes. I think of nothing, I remember
        nothing, I just listen to the sound it makes.

She   You know, you've very interesting to talk to.

He   Really?

She   *(thoughtfully)* We have no one like you in our circus. Though when
        I first saw you, you reminded me awfully of a poodle I knew.
        Grumpy but beautifully trained. Mind you by then he'd stopped
        performing. He just travelled with the circus.

He   I'm sorry, why had he stopped performing?

She   His age. He wasn't any good anymore.

He   I see. Thank you very much.

She   No, no, don't be offended. You're quite different. You're very active,
        you enjoy life.

He   You think so?

She   I'm sure you do. Only don't you get bored, living alone?

He   There you go again! I'm sorry but that's really very funny. I live
        absolutely surrounded by people. Too many in fact. The per-
        sonalities I meet, the lives I get involved in. Every one of my patients
        is to me an open book, a living book which I read with the utmost
        interest. You might think they were strangers. But when you get
        involved as a doctor, they become part of you. When you talk of my
        loneliness, you don't know what you're talking about.

She   There, you're angry again.

He   *(grumpy)* I'm not a bit angry.

She   Yes, you are. You're angry.

He   I'm not, damn it! Though women invariably make you angry if you
        talk to them long enough.

She   Poor women, why are you so against them?

He   First because they're bad patients. You simply can't compare a
        woman and a man who don't feel well. Second ... But that's private.

She   And third?

He   Also private.

She   I hope you didn't get so angry with your wife? *(Pause)* Why don't
        you answer me?

He   *(quietly)* My wife was a marvellous woman. *(Smiles and adds after
        a slight pause)* Marvellous.

She   *(very quietly)* Where is she now?

He looks carefully in every direction and shrugs rather helplessly.

I see. She went away and left you.

He   That's right. She left me.

She   And have you never, never really loved anyone since?

He   *(with a wry smile)* Well, there was one dreadful occasion when I took it into my head to marry.

She   And then what?

He   I was horrified.

She   Why?

He   Incompatibility. Not worth it. Stupid.

She   *(even somehow surprised)* But I understand that. What has been cannot be replaced. No one could. Everyone else seems worthless, pathetic, stupid.

He   *(passionately)* Exactly. Word for word.

She   Surprise! We agree!

He   You think so?

She   There, it's raining again.

He   Yes, raining hard.

She   Awfully hard.

He   Let's stand in the doorway.

She   No, no! I'm afraid.

He   There's nothing to be afraid of.

She   What do you mean, nothing? It's crazy but I am afraid.

He   How absurd. You are an amazing woman.

She   No, I'm not. I'm just afraid . . .

He   Well then, I'll open my umbrella.

She   Go on, don't talk about it. Open it quickly. Heavens, how slow he is. We'll be drenched.

He   *(opens his umbrella)* If you hurry, you could break it. Now take hold of the handle.

She   I have.

He   All right now?

She   Not bad.

He   It's an excellent umbrella. Nice and roomy. You know, it's rather snug under here.

She   What a thing to enjoy!

He   Why not?

She   There was a time when I loved rain. God, I was mad about it! Wonderful ideas in the rain popped into my head. I jumped in and out of puddles and I hated umbrellas. But now I've aged, I'm afraid. I suppose I'm afraid of catching cold. I hurry, hurry, in the most pathetic way, to get under an umbrella. God, how humiliating!

He   What's humiliating about it?

She   The disgusting speed with which I seek shelter. My cowardice is humiliating. I tell you what, let's break the umbrella!

He   Why?

She   We'll break it! We'll put up a fight, we won't give in!

He   To what?

She   To old age. That's what! Of course it's old age! But we won't give in! We'll break the umbrella and stand bare-headed under the rain! As we did when we were young! We'll break this idiotic stick in two, damn it!

He   What are you doing? Stop!

She   *(closes the umbrella)* I'll smash it over my knee! One! Eh-eh . . . Not easy . . . *(Notices him swaying and losing his balance)* What's the matter with you?

He   Nothing. I must sit down. On this step.

She   Why?

He   I'll feel better.

She   Don't you feel well?

He   It's nothing. *(Finds some pills and swallows one)* It happens.

She   Heart? *(He nods)* How awful. And you have no one to look after you.

He   What's your name?

She   Zherber.

He   I don't mean that. Your name?

She   Lidya Vasilyevna . . . Lida. Why?

He   I wanted to know.

She   Why?

He   I'm not sure.

She   *(horrified)* The steps you're sitting on are wet!

He   I'm wearing a raincoat. It's quite snug. It's really rather nice.

She   Are you feeling better?

He   Not yet. In a moment. You'll see.

She   Hurry up.

He   Has it stopped raining?

She   Yes.

He   Where's my umbrella?

She   Lying over there in a puddle.

He   Have you broken it?

She   I couldn't.

He   What wonderful news. *(Sighs)* Well now . . . I think it has let go of me now. *(Raises his head and looks around)* Just look at that.

She   What?

He   *(wonder-struck)* Lidya Vasilyevna, Lida, it's wonderful to be alive.

SCENE FOUR

Her fifteenth day.

Hospital on the outskirts of Riga. A bright sunny morning. In the garden Rodion Nikolayevich has settled on a bench with a book. He wears hospital pyjamas and a white linen cap to protect him from the sun.

Lidya Vasilyevna appears on the garden path. She carries a bag. Seeing him, she stands still and looks at him fixedly as though studying him. He raises his head and notices her.

He   *(infinitely surprised)* Lidya Vasilyevna?

She   *(reminding him gently)* Lida.

He   Yes, yes, I'm sorry, Lida. What are you doing here?

She   You see, I was going past the hospital quite by chance and then all of a sudden I stopped by the gate. Then I suddenly remembered you've been in the Rheumocardiac department here for four days. Velta Radzika, the duty sister, told me. She's been quite agreeable to me lately. As I was going past the hospital by chance, on an impulse I decided to inquire how you were. You see I feel guilty. I keep wondering if it was because of me that you were brought here, if it's my fault that you're in such a catastrophic condition.

He   *(drily)* First, my condition is not catastrophic and it isn't going to be. Second, my heart does play me up a bit as you saw. And third and last, I've simply been advised a few days change of scenery.

She   Excellent! I'm glad you've recovered so quickly.

He   I repeat, I have not been ill. So there is no question of my recovery. I feel perfectly well and in a few days I'll be back at work.

She   That's fine. But have you some kind of glass jar you could put these carnations in? I don't know why I bought them. *(She takes some carnations out of her bag and cautiously hands them to him)*

He   Oh, well, then . . . *(Almost excited)* Yes, I'll find a glass jar. I assure you, Lidya Vasilyevna, that I'll find something.

She   *(gently)* Lida.

He   Yes, yes, I'm sorry.

She   By the way, is the food any good here?

He   I can't honestly say I enjoy the cooking. You know, hospital food, rather tasteless.

She   In that case, perhaps you'll try a little of my broth. I happened to be cooking some this morning with Velta Radzika, the one who's being so nice to me.

He   *(grumpy)* First, I can't imagine why you're spoiling me. *(Mildly)*

	Second, I think I will try your broth. Frankly I rather miss home cooking. *(Tries the broth)*
She	*(holding her breath)* Well?
He	*(slight pause)* Why haven't you told me the truth?
She	What do you mean?
He	*(thoughtful)* You're not a cashier.
She	*(frightened)* Why not?
He	You're a cook. A remarkable cook.
She	*(excited)* In that case I don't suppose you'll mind eating these three little chops. I happen to have them in my bag.
He	I shall drink the soup and then I shall eat the chops. Healthy men have healthy appetites.
She	While you're eating, will it cheer you up if I tell you that I'm getting on very well with my neighbours now. Some of them even go walking with me in the garden at night and the more energetic ones have actually watched the sunrise. And we don't make any noise climbing through the window because Velta Radzika, who's so nice to me, has given us a key to the front door.
He	But don't you realize—you start with a minor infringement and next thing you're leading a mass movement?
She	Does it matter? You know, now in the morning, they simply beg me to sing them something. And a few join in.
He	I hope the rest of the wing is comparatively quiet?
She	I'm not sure. But a lot fewer of them are late for breakfast. *(With interest)* What do you think of the chops? I see you've started on the second.
He	The delicate flavour of garlic shows they were prepared by a culinary expert.
She	I'm awfully glad. My husband likes my cooking too. *(Slight pause)* Tell me, what has become of your beloved umbrella? You know, it has occurred to me that perhaps your indisposition was brought on by your fear of losing it for ever.
He	*(unexpectedly gentle)* Well, it's an old friend that umbrella. No one likes to see an old friend battered to death. No, no, it's nothing to do with that. My heart does play me up. After all, I fought in two wars and fantastic wars at that.
She	Surely you weren't old enough to fight in the Civil War?
He	Yes, I fought against the White Army outside Petrograd. Fifteen I was. We fought against trained Tsarist troops supplied with arms by the Allies. We had one rifle between three men. The one who survived got it. I survived all right. My friends were killed beside me and I could do nothing to help them. I suppose that's what made me want to be a doctor—a surgeon. So, next thing, off I went—medical student. The arguments we used to have! We read Mayakovsky. We fought over Essenin, Meyerhold, and we were violent against the New Economic Policy.

She   Oh, the Nepmen!

He   We were always hungry, always poor and so cold! Once I came home and found a rat in my bed, trying to keep warm, I suppose. But we had fun, you know.

She   They wouldn't understand now.

He   There's a lot they wouldn't understand. Sometimes I think I'm a dinosaur. I walk down the street, I look about me and I know I'm a a dinosaur. A mammoth.

She   I was a student too. I was studying for the theatre. I was an actress before I was a cashier. Don't you believe me? With our student group we toured all the big construction sites—Magnitka, Dneproguess. God, what hopes we had!

He   I went charging all over the country too. During the first five year plan when anything started anywhere, I was there on a mission or expedition of some kind. Now I can't even imagine what I was like.

She   I can see you vividly discussing whether a member of the Young Communist League should wear a tie or not.

He   I bet you were pretty lively in those days!

She   I certainly was. I was even afraid of myself! In the summer we took a house in the country. There were Nepmen next door. Every night I appeared in their garden in a white bedspread. I played the ghost. They left their house in the middle of July. Scared out of their wits.

He   How old were you on that famous occasion?

She   Fourteen. Three years later I married. And a year later I had a son.

He   So young? I don't believe it.

She   Yes, it's true . . . (Smiles) We called him Petya.

He   And your husband, was he always an artiste?

She   No, no! I had quite another husband then. Nothing in common! Well, I had to marry several times. But all that was before the war. Later I had more sense. I took myself in hand. After the war I only married once.

He   You know, you're dangerous!

She   Not now, Rodion Nikolayevich . . . not now.

He   And your first husband, what was he?

She   Snezhinsky? Neither this nor that. Like testing a nib to see how it writes. After Petya was born, I had no more use for him.

He   Perhaps Petya might have had a use for him?

She   Snezhinsky? He was a born fool. Petya would have guessed that in his cradle. It would have been traumatic for him. And he would have hated me for providing him with a fool of a father.

He   Why did you marry him?

She   Why? I was madly in love with him, of course.

He   (getting angry) What for?

She   How should I know! No one ever knows that. Well, some people pretend they do. It makes them feel better. But I've always been

absolutely frank with myself. I looked truth straight in the eye—
Snezhinsky was a fool.

He   This is a nightmare!

She   Now, my dear, please don't be upset. It's bad for you, now, please . . .
I'm a reformed character. Quite another person, not a bit flighty.
Twenty years ago I married for the last time! And I still love him,
tenderly and loyally.

He   Tenderly and loyally?

She   Tenderly and loyally. Now do you feel better?

He   A bit better. *(Slight pause)* Twenty years is something.

She   You see. *(Slight pause)* Have you loved your wife a long time?

He   *(thinks)* All my life I think.

She   *(surprised and envious)* All your life? That's interesting, of course.

He   I once carried her for eight kilometres.

She   Why?

He   I don't know. I wanted to.

She   What for?

He   Oh, fun.

She   What about her?

He   She fell asleep.

She   The ingratitude!

He   No, not at all. A few months later we had a little girl.

She   Oh, I see, that's different.

He   For ten years we'd had no children. It was funny and sad. And
suddenly there was a dear little girl, Katya. A month and a half later
the war started.

She   My Petya was almost grown up. He was fourteen. He was very
handsome. And completely independent. He used to laugh a lot.
He'd take one look at me and burst out laughing. "Now why are you
laughing?" I'd say, "it's embarrassing." "Because you're so funny,"
he'd say. "How can I be funny," I'd say, "they always cast me in
drama and tragedy?" "That's because you're a good actress," he'd
say, "and they just don't know how funny you are." And then he'd
start kissing me.

He   Does he still live with you?

She   You know, at a very early age he loved sitting-in at rehearsals. And
we were all amazed at some of his comments. When he was twelve
he wrote an epic drama. "The Slaves' Uprising." It wasn't at all bad
for his age. Later he burnt it. When I protested, he assured me that
Gogol had done the same thing.

He   Where is he now?

She   He hasn't been around for a long time now. *(Smiles guiltily)* He
was killed at Koenigsberg. Right at the end of the war. He was only
eighteen. It was so embarrassing because I was at the front in a
show for the troops. Near Berlin. Just next door. It was Victory Day.

We were celebrating. I was very happy. *(Suddenly in a whisper)* I
didn't know.

He   *(after a long pause)* Was he the only child?

     She smiles and nods.

Pity.

She   He had been bursting to go to the front. Because he had a very
patriotic upbringing, you know. He had an extraordinary love of his
country. He was a very good boy. *(Looks at Rodion Nikolayevich
and laughs barely audibly)* I'm talking too much . . . talking and
talking, forgetting you're ill, but, of course, I know you're really
quite fit. *(Rises from the bench)* Now I'm going into Riga to the
circus. An old friend of mine is taking part in the Stunts of Icarus.
She and her husband separated recently. It's very sad. *(Somewhat
busy and embarrassed about it, she takes a box of sweets from her
bag)* I quite forgot. *(Holds the box out to him)* Your favourites.

He   *(very excited)* Thank you, thank you very much . . . What have I done
to deserve all this?

She   If I don't, who will? *(Goes quickly)*

     Curtain

PART TWO

SCENE ONE

Her eighteenth day.

*Rest-room in the sanatorium. Dusk. Lidya Vasilyevna, her
legs tucked under her like a child, is sitting in an armchair
by a standard lamp with the light on. From next door where
the television is on comes the sound of voices and music.
Outside the rain is pouring down. There is thunder and a
gale blowing from the sea.*

She   *(sings quietly and thoughtfully):*
    "In many countries I have been
    My squirrel and I . . ."

     *Rodion Nikolayevich looks in at the door, sees her, stops
     and listens to her.*

(notices him) It's you! You're back? In this rain! Have you quite,
quite recovered?

He   *(significantly)* I've had a marvellous rest.

She   *(hastily)* Yes, yes, of course.

He   Look, I got you some carnations . . . Three. *(He gives her the flowers)*

She   Really? How remarkable.

He   Why are you alone?

She   They've all gone to a concert. Some are sitting by the television set. I'm sitting here thinking and listening to the rain. *(Looks at him)* I knew you'd be back today. I was quite sure you would.

He   Why?

She   I don't know. *(Pause)* There's a storm at sea. A fantastic storm. I was out in it. Not a soul on the beach. A bathing-hut was washed away and there's lightning! Actually I couldn't stick it for long. First, I was drenched and then I was afraid.

He   I don't know. I don't know . . . Behaving like this at your age is just absurd.

She   You do go on about my age. Do you know what a wise Frenchman said? Growing old is boring but that's the only way to a long life.

He   There's nothing special about a long life. An interesting life—that's what counts.

She   Well, has your life been interesting in these last few days?

He   Oh, very. I spent every morning dreaming about your soup.

She   That's nothing! You should taste my stuffed cabbage-leaves. My husband goes into raptures usually. *(Pause)* I keep thinking of my departure. I've had over half my stay here. Funny! I'll be a long way away and you'll be here as usual walking about, thinking your thoughts . . . Funny.

He   What's funny?

She   Though of course, I shall have masses of interesting things to do when I get back to Moscow.

He   What sort of things?

She   Oh, this and that. I've decided to redecorate! I'm going to change the wallpaper. I love redecorating; it doesn't tire me at all. I move the furniture around, making a whole new room. The bed where the table was . . . It's very amusing. *(Vivacious)* If you like, I'll move everything round for you.

He   *(cheerful)* You're too late! I have just finished redecorating my daughter's room. Literally only a few days ago. And I've changed the wallpaper too. I'm so looking forward to seeing her. She and her husband work in Japan for our trade delegation there. It's funny, I live here and she lives among the Japs. But her leave is due any day now, thank God. *(Laughs)* Only I can't work out the exact date.

She   Yes, we all have our problems. Mine are nothing serious. But do you know what I worry about at night?

He   No, I'd like to know.

She   I've brought such a lovely dress. Extraordinarily becoming; and it fits me perfectly. But I haven't been able to wear it. There's absolutely nowhere to go! I did think of wearing it to the museum but I changed my mind just in time. Say what you like, a museum does require something formal. But it's rather . . . No, no, not outrageous, but . . . It's humiliating, it's so humiliating to take it back without having worn it, it's just awful! But you wouldn't understand, you're not a woman

He   No, that's right. *(Cautious)* When you get back to Moscow, couldn't you wear it to the opera or the ballet?

She   Yes, but, it's a pity, it's a pity to take it back unworn! Especially as here it would be a sensation. I'm willing to bet it would be a sensation.

He   Couldn't you wear it to one of our social evenings?

She   No, no, I couldn't possibly attract attention here in the sanatorium. It would be tactless. *(Slight pause)* Do you ever go to restaurants?

He   No, I don't really care for eating out. I much prefer home cooking.

She   You don't understand. Food is not the point. I mentioned a restaurant as a place where you can enjoy yourself, dancing, drinking, champagne . . . you know what I mean.

He   I don't think I do.

She   Well, in a restaurant, you can wear a new hair-style. Or put on a suit you've never worn before.

He   No, honestly, I can't say I've any feelings like that. I haven't been in a restaurant for years. I've never had a new hair-style. *(Thinks)* But when you get back to Moscow your husband after all this time will enjoy taking you out.

She   Well, it's unlikely. Though we shall be back there at the same time. Curious coincidence, don't you think? I expect we shall meet. Though he's terribly busy when he is in Moscow.

He   You seem to have a very peculiar relationship with your husband?

She   Marriage is a very peculiar phenomenon. Getting married is easy; it's staying married that's difficult. *(Slight pause)* By the way, are you aware who my husband is? He's a famous musical eccentric.

He   Well, how incredibly lucky for you. Marriage to a musical eccentric must be the height of happiness.

She   *(severe)* That is not funny. My husband is a man of extraordinary talent. A subtle artiste, a wonderful musician. It's impossible to describe the impact he made when he was young. I was stunned the first time I saw him. He played an enormous trumpet, that big, and little accordions, that small, at one and the same time. At one and the same time, you know! The audience wept with delight. It's easy to imagine how I fell in love with him for ever! I was still in my thirties—almost a girl . . . Besides I was terribly disillusioned with the theatre. I'll tell you why some other time. So I left the theatre and followed him everywhere. He was so gentle, kind, considerate. He saw that I too needed success and applause. After all I was an actress, he realized it perfectly. And then we did an act together.

(Delighted) I wore a wonderful costume: a silver cape, pink tights and an ash-blonde wig. The orchestra struck up, I bowed and sang my opening number:
(she sings the Song of the Circus):

Ta-rum, ta-ray, throw every care away!
Forget it all and join us in the circus.
No frowns, no fears, but laughter, fun and cheers,
For you and I and they all love the circus.

How very wise this elephant.
He knows the show from ring to rafter.
And whilst we're here, we're sacrosanct!
The circus is in love with life and laughter.

The spangled gowns, the conjurers and clowns,
The horses' nodding plumes will all delight you;
Artistes who act work hard and that's a fact
At circus tricks created to excite you.

The circus tent is wide and high
To hold our glitter and our daring.
The big parade of talent passes by—
The acrobats, the band with music blaring.

But you'll forget those pleasant times we met;
The artiste's voice, her eyes, the song she sang you,
The parts she played—yes, all will quickly fade,
Except her lingering memories of you.

While we are here and we exist
We are the wonder of the circus;
While we remain, we'll always be the same:
The wonder and the magic of the circus.

He   Yes, of course. I'm sorry I never saw that act. I suppose there is no hope of seeing it now!

She   Oh, it's only a memory, only a memory. You can't imagine how grateful I am to my husband. I had my greatest success in the circus. Entirely due to him. Believe me, he is a wonderful artiste. And generous too.

He   Judging by what you say, it seems a pity you don't see more of him.

She   What can I do? What can I do about it? You see, for quite a long time now my husband has been married to another woman.

He   *(shaken)* Married? What do you mean?

She   It's quite simple. Married—that's all. There's nothing I can do about it.

He   But what the hell!

She   Do you think so? *(Feebly)* I don't know. On the other hand, what was he to do?

He	Do?
She	Ten years ago he met a woman he fell madly in love with. What's wrong with that? Can you blame him for falling in love with her? I can't! After all I was considerably older than he was. And say what you like, a middle-aged woman isn't nearly as attractive as a young woman. You agree with that, don't you?
He	No! I don't!
She	*(reasonably)* Now don't let's forget he fell in love with her. Love is sacred. Imagine yourself in his position.
He	Certainly not!
She	You're very unreasonable. Not at all contemporary. In fact you surprise me. He behaved beautifully towards me. Beautifully. He never deceived me. Never. He came and announced quite openly: "You know, Lidakins, I'm in love with another woman." He was almost in tears.
He	Well, I'll be damned!
She	For a time we even went on with our act. Of course, there were difficulties. When we went on tour, the three of us had to travel together, which affected our morale. It was all right in the end. She took my place in the circus ring. She did the act beautifully. Mind you, we had to rehearse her very carefully. And so she was a great success too. Actually I was sorry to alter my lovely costume to fit her, my silver cape, for instance, but then, what can you do . . .
He	I think it would be a good idea to shoot her.
She	What do you mean? She's very musical and she has rhythm. She put over my opening song—the one I just sang you—very creditably and with sparkle. Of course, it wasn't quite perfect. But then she has a wonderful figure, like a goddess. And she treats me quite well. I can't complain. And above all, she's very devoted to my husband. Quite devoted! I don't think she'll ever be unfaithful to him.
He	So it was after this that you became a cashier in the circus?
She	Certainly not! It was some time before I gave in, let me tell you. I put my own act together. People congratulated me! And do you know, I went on in the ring for nearly a month.
He	What happened then?
She	You see, it wasn't a great success. So, in due course, my friends had me transferred to the box-office, because actually I'm a practical person. Incredible luck, don't you think? I do so love the circus.

> *Deeply moved he says nothing, then takes her hand and kisses it respectfully.*

(snatching her hand away) You make a great mistake if you're sorry for me. I'm on excellent terms with my husband. Thank God if everyone were the same! Why, two months ago, before he went to the Caspian, he borrowed a hundred and fifty roubles from me. He may even pay it back. Everything's possible, everything!

Very angry she runs out of the room.

He is confused and remains standing there. The rain continues beating on the window-panes.

She   *(she returns)* What a downpour! What a downpour!

He   *(gently)* Don't be upset, please don't.

She   I wanted to tell you something else but I forget what it was.

He   I have a suggestion to make. I would like to invite you, one evening as soon as possible, to come and have dinner with me, at a restaurant. I don't think we'll tell any of my colleagues or any of the other patients . . . I mean, people staying here. I wonder, would Tuesday suit you?

Lightning. Thunder.

SCENE TWO

Her twenty-first day.

A small garden by the entrance to a summer-restaurant. It is fairly late. The sky is full of stars. The weather is good. There comes the sound of music from the restaurant. The door opens. Lidya Vasilyevna and Rodion Nikolayevich come down the steps. They're enjoying themselves.

She   I think it's rather late.

He   I think it's terribly late.

She   You have a funny sort of laugh.

He   What luck no one spotted us.

She   Great luck. *(Slight pause)* But it would have been interesting if someone from the sanatorium had come into the restaurant.

He   Terrible.

She   Especially when you tried that trick with the glasses.

He   A momentary weakness.

She   Don't worry, your patients are peacefully asleep. *(Surprised)* Why are you beating time in such a peculiar manner?

He   I'm trying to remember where I left my hat.

She   You've got it in your hand.

He   At last I've found it!

She   Put it on your head. Everything will fall into place.

He   *(puts it on)* You're right. That's a lot better. *(Thinks)* Why don't we go somewhere?

She   Because we like it here.

He   Then why aren't we sitting on that bench?

She   Because we're just going to.

They sit on the bench.

He   That's it! We've done it—we've displayed your finery to the whole world.

She   Do you like it?

He   Wildly. I'm almost blinded.

She   The champagne was very good.

He   Yes. The champagne was excellent. An entirely different view of life has opened up before me. There was a moment in there when I actually said to myself—well, well, well . . .

She   It was well said.

He   I never thought I could enjoy myself so much.

She   And it's madly good for you. Enjoyment is a guarantee of health. Please stick that slogan on your surgery door.

He   They'd remove it.

She   Would they?

He   First the slogan, then me.

She   They wouldn't dare!

He   Oh, wouldn't they just?

She   Well, then, let's round them up and shoot them.

He   They wouldn't agree to that. *(Thinks)* Wouldn't it be a better idea to take the boat to Tallin.

She   They wouldn't understand.

He   What a pity. *(Pause)* The night is so cool.

She   And the sky is full of stars.

He   That means rain.

She   I don't mind. I like everything here—rain, sun, storms, stars.

He   Is that poetry?

She   Could be.

He   Let's take the boat to Piarna.

She   We can't. That would upset them.

He   That's terrible.

She   We'll get over it. There are lots of nice people here.

He   Possibly. But their dancing is very peculiar. Did you notice?

She   I had a good look. It was very crowded.

He   There was someone dressed in a fringe crawling round my legs. I don't know what he was up to.

She   That's the Twist—you're simply out of touch.

He   I had an awful shock. There he was all of a sudden, right under my feet.

She   You get used to it.

He   Do you think so? *(Embarrassed)* Well, I haven't been in a restaurant for years. *(Does not want to appear reactionary)* Anyway we've taken a great step forward somewhere.

She   There's a theory, the Twist began with television. You sit in an armchair for so long you get ossified. So you have to get up, move around, get unstuck. A few light movements *(she demonstrates the basic movements of the Twist)* and the tension is gone. But the Twist is out of fashion.

He   Really? I find that very encouraging. But the other dances are just as surprising. *(Listens to the music)* Now, take that one. They all wave their arms in every direction and it puts me on my guard.

She   There I disagree with you! The Shake gives us our individuality back again. *(Listening to the music, she sketches in the Shake as it were, turning it into something unpremeditated and eccentric)* You see, I'm free, I'm light. I'm expressing myself. I'm improvising!

Ends her dance with the orchestra which stops playing.

Well, how was that?

He   Very nice. And rather disgraceful.

She   You're hopeless. Conformist! Peripatetic do-gooder—that's what you are! I can imagine the stick-in-the-mud you must have been when you were young.

He   Let me tell you that at the height of the first five year plan, I danced the Lezguinka and Kamarinska till I dropped. Actually out of protest against the depraved Shimmy and that Charleston.

She   What? You never did the Shimmy?

He   Yes, I did. And the Charleston. But that never stopped me from condemning them.

She   Hypocrite! No, I shall never believe you could do the Charleston. The Charleston requires elegance, abandon, joy!

He   *(obstinate)* I tell you I did.

She   Prove it.

He   What?

She   Here. Now. This moment.

He   I'll prove it.

She   Go on ... *(He gets up)* Right, wait ... First ... No, you've got to get your feet going the right way ... *(With decision)* I can't. I can't do it like this.

She   Why not?

He   I've no accompaniment.

She   Don't despair, here you are. *(Hums an old Charleston tune, clapping in time)*

He   That's it. That's it.

She   Come on, now. You're not much good.

He tries harder and does a few steps, some of which are

distantly reminiscent of the Charleston and others of the Lezguinka.

He   Hang on, something's happening. It's coming back. Louder! Louder!

She   We'll be arrested.

He   Who cares! *(With some panache and more confidence he has abandoned decorum)* Well?

She   You're improving but I'm not bowled over.

He   *(stops dancing)* I know. The Charleston is made for two.

She   *(on her guard)* What do you mean?

He   I can't do it alone.

She   You don't mean . . .

He   Of course.

She   But the police? The vigilantes?

He   Too late. There's no stopping me now!

She   Eh! Then let it rip!

They dance. Of course it is far from perfect, but gradually they sort themselves out.

She   One, two, one, two.

He   Aha! You see, we're dancing.

She   Gently! Don't jump like that. And don't kick so much! Where's your sense of rhythm? Remember, elegance . . . That's enough. Enough.

They stop dancing.

He   I think some of it worked.

She   Up to a point.

He   There you see, I did do the Charleston.

She   I suppose so. But a very long time ago.

He   Forty years ago! Of course I may have forgotten some of the details, but not the general outline.

She   Well . . .

He   I also did the Shimmy!

She   Oh God! Think of your heart.

He   I'm not going to.

She   You dare-devil!

He   When I dance, I dance!

She   We're done for!

Accompanying themselves, they do the Shimmy, in which they are rather more successful.

He   *(dancing)* There you are, I can do the Shimmy too . . .

She   You mustn't shake so much.

He   But you have to shake in the Shimmy.

She   Not so much. Just a little. A little—that's the trick of it.
He   All right—I can shake a little . . .

They do it quite well.

She   Enough . . .

They stop.

He   You're pretty good.
She   We really must get our breath back.
He   You've a point there.

They settle themselves on the bench with pleasure.

She   God, how lovely.
He   Couldn't be better.
She   We've done awfully well.
He   I think so too. *(Pause)* Say what you like but the Shimmy and the Charleston were far superior to those modern dances.
She   Then why did you protest against them so passionately?
He   How was I to know they'd be so worth while after all?
She   Yes, isn't life gorgeous.
He   Let's take the boat to Kaunas.
She   We mustn't. It might look bad.
He   Why? Surely we're too old for them to think that.
She   Do you think so?
He   *(glances at her)* Damn it, you're dangerous.
She   Not to you. You forget, you're a m-m-misogynist.
He   Quite right. *(With heat)* Are there any women left in the world now with whom one could in any way compare. No vanished!
She   Or any men with whom one could in any way compare . . . vanished!
He   The men have vanished and the woman have vanished.
She   They've all vanished.
He   Now that's terrible.
She   But we don't mind. Because we remember.
He   That's right. And that is enough for us.
She   *(suddenly)* You think so?
He   Do you?
She   Me? I don't know. I think so. Yes.
He   Me too. I think so.
She   Now that's good. We both think so.
He   We think so and that's that.
She   But there are people who say they're afraid of loneliness.
He   Does one have to be afraid!
She   I'm not afraid . . .

He   Funny though. Sometimes, towards evening, one grows a little sad.
She   Well, perhaps just a little . . .
He   Slightly, slightly.
She   Just the teeniest bit.

> *The restaurant orchestra strikes up a slow waltz. They get up. He puts his arm round her waist. She smiles and slowly they go waltzing round and round till they waltz off.*

SCENE THREE

Her twenty-third day.

The sun has just set on the sea. Rodion Nikolayevich and Lidya Vasilyevna are slowly strolling down a path between pine trees.

He   Why are you laughing? No, why? You've been silent for a long time and now you're laughing.
She   We've done remarkably well.
He   Do you really think so?
She   We've been wandering about for over an hour and we just keep going.
He   Yes. It's all so new to me. Watching that sunset, for instance.
She   That was a unique success.
He   Possibly. But where is it all leading to? I'm heading straight for the abyss. Two days ago outside a restaurant I danced the Charleston.
She   Yes, it was quite a show.
He   The horror of it! I keep remembering our excesses and shuddering.
She   Why? It was all so nice. And so unexpected of you.
He   Supposing someone had spotted us. One of my staff?
She   What sort of head are you, if you're afraid of responsibility?
He   To listen to you . . .
She   Do listen. We haven't got much longer. And where have you been all day?
He   At the hospital in town. I was operating.
She   Really?
He   I'm a surgeon. I keep my hand in. One must in case there's a war. *(With an ironic smile)* Anything can happen.
She   Anything?
He   Who knows?
She   *(pause)* It's awful.
He   It is.

They come to a war-cemetery. It is right by the sea, where the road bends slightly away from the pine trees. Laid on the graves are rectangular slabs of marble inscribed with the names of the dead. Above them is a bas-relief of three soldiers' helmets in sandstone.

She   I've been here before.

He   Let's go. Don't let's stay.

She   Why not?

He   There's no point.

She   You surprise me.

He says nothing.

What a strange place to choose for a cemetery. Right by the sea.

He   There was a lot of fighting here in October forty-four. Terrible losses. *(Pause)* They died here, by the sea, on this ground, and they were buried here.

She   Did you fight here?

He   No.

She   Then how do you know?

He   I heard about it.

She   All this has happened. Remembering makes one afraid.

He   One has to remember.

She   Those who died?

He   Them too.

She   Do you think it will happen again?

He   We must live in such a way that it doesn't.

She   *(looks at him gratefully)* That's right. *(Slight pause)* I'm tired. *(Sits on the bench)*

He   Never mind. *(He sits next to her)*

She   Do you remember, I promised to tell you why I left the theatre? Well, it was after Petya's death. After Victory Day. I can't explain it. But in the war-plays—and we had a lot of those—when I heard shooting off-stage, I felt ashamed because I was an actress. Death and grief were only make-believe on the stage. That's where art should stop short. Because I couldn't pretend. And I left the theatre. *(Pause)* The circus was different. Everyone laughed and enjoyed themselves. That saved me.

He   That's difficult for me to understand.

She   I know. My friends couldn't either. I suppose I'm a coward. But what can I do. *(Pause)* Why are you smiling?

He   I was thinking of the first moment I saw you.

She   And . . . ?

He   I almost burst out laughing. No, no, not that you were funny. I just felt happy all of a sudden.

She   I really don't know. Should I feel pleased about that.

He   *(pause)* Are you going away the day after tomorrow?

She   Yes. *(Smiles)* It's time.

He   *(in confusion)* But I've got used to you.

She   *(astonished without showing it)* You'll get used without me.

He   I suppose so.

She   *(angry)* Does that please you?

He   No . . . It makes me sad. It does—I mean it. Though that's silly of course.

She   But why is it silly?

He   I don't know. It's just silly, that's all. All right! Damn it! After all I'm used to living alone. No one to get bored with.

She   Don't be angry because I ask you but you've never told me and I've never understood why your wife left you. What happened?

He   *(not loudly)* The war.

She   Well?

He   She went off into the army. And she never came back. *(Smiles)* And that's all. That's how it was. It's all very simple.

She   *(quietly)* All right, if you don't want to talk about it . . .

He   I wasn't talking about it. You asked me. *(Slight pause)* Though why shouldn't I talk about it? There's no point in keeping quiet about her. She was a surgeon like me. When there's a war, a surgeon's place is at the front. That's obvious. We were sent to different fronts and we didn't meet after forty-one. She was twice wounded and twice she went back. In forty-four she . . . ceased to exist. They killed her. For three years she'd lived without me. *(Thinks)* Perhaps she'd changed? I don't know. But I must not forget her. It would be unthinkable. *(Pause)* When I got back to Leningrad after the war I kept thinking she was alive. I'd be walking down the street and I'd suddenly think: she's at home waiting for me. My daughter was six years old. We had fun together but we both thought of her.

She   Why did you leave Leningrad? It's your home town. Don't you like it?

He   Yes, I do.

She   Then why did you leave?

He   Oh, it just happened.

She   But you could go back?

He   No.

She   Why not?

He   *(almost rude)* I couldn't—that's all.

She   *(quietly)* Were you very happy? *(Touches his hand)* Before the war?

He   I suppose so.

She   Was I or wasn't I happy? I don't know. I had fun, I know that. I don't suppose there are any really happy people. You don't often see them, do you? Though ... I once watched a very happy couple. I came across them late one evening in a street in old Moscow. They were walking fairly slowly—they were really very old, but so neatly dressed and friendly ... He was leading her carefully by the arm and at the same time they were laughing an awful lot. *(Thinks)* Since then I have never seen a happier couple.

He   And you envied them?

She   *(quietly)* Yes.

He   I think I'd have envied them.

She   They were walking along propping each other up. And they were having such fun.

He   Don't take it personally but, you know, loyalty is the greatest form of strength.

She   Yes. *(Thinks)* It may be. *(Looks at him)* It may be. *(She looks round)* I often come here. I don't know why. In celebration, perhaps. At the same time you feel such pain deep down—it's quite unbearable. *(She approaches and reads the graves to him)* "Pyotr Akimov. Sergeant in the Tank Corps. Born nineteen twenty-four. Died twenty-third of October nineteen forty-four." He was only twenty ... *(Looks at another grave)* There are always fresh flowers on this grave. It's extraordinary. Someone comes here every day. *(She reads)* "Nina Semyonova, Major of the Medical Corps. Born nineteen twelve—died twenty-fifth of October nineteen forty-four." She was in her thirties. She'd be getting on now. *(Picks up a flower and smells it)* They're fresh. Someone put them here this morning.

He   *(quietly)* Don't touch them.

> Suddenly coming awake as it were, she stares at him, hesitating to ask him why. He does not reply for some time and then he gives a barely perceptible nod.

She   Oh God ... Forgive me.

He   *(smiles)* For what?

She   I keep laughing ... joking all the time.

He   That's all right.

She   *(seeing it all in a flash)* So that's why you live here

He   It's dark. Let's go.

> Without saying a word, she runs away quickly.

SCENE FOUR

Her twenty-sixth day.

Afternoon. A slight drizzle. Under an umbrella Lidya Vasilyevna is sitting on her suitcase by the iron gates of the sanatorium. She is dressed very simply for travelling with a kerchief on her head. Her second suitcase stands beside her. There is also a shopping bag with apples.

She   *(sings very quietly)*
       "In many countries I have been,
       My squirrel and I . . ."

       Rodion Nikolayevich appears by the gates. She sees him, stops singing and looks at him.

He   You can close your umbrella. It's stopped raining.

She   Really?

He   Aren't you ashamed of yourself?

She   *(feebly)* Ashamed? Why?

He   I've been looking for you everywhere.

She   Have you?

He   Where have you been?

She   When?

He   These last two days we haven't seen each other.

She   I've been going on long excursions.

He   That is not true. You've been hiding.

She   I have not been hiding. I simply decided to spend my last few days visiting places. *(With spirit)* Well, why shouldn't I visit places?

He   What are you doing here? Skulking in that absurd garment, sitting on your suitcases! With a bag of apples.

She   I'm leaving. I've called a taxi. My husband adores apples.

He   But the day has only just started. And the Moscow train doesn't go till evening.

She   I decided to spend my last few hours in Riga. And go and say good-bye to my favourite patisserie with its delicious apple-tarts.

He   That's fine! You can say good-bye to the patisserie, but you can't spare time to say good-bye to me! You knew I was operating this morning so you decided to sneak out of the sanatorium.

She   *(innocently)* I did not sneak out! God knows, I signed the form. I shook hands with everyone, I said good-bye . . .

He   Why haven't you said good-bye to me?

She   I didn't want to.

He   Why not?

She   I don't know. Quite a lot of my actions are not at all clear to me
        (Pause) Anyway as from today, my stay here is over . . .

He   You told me you had ten more days. Your circus doesn't open til
        the first of September. And I could easily extend your treatment fo
        another week.

She   Why?

He   (muddling along) Well, you aren't strong enough . . . Your arterio
        sclerosis . . .

She   (in some triumph) Too late! I've signed out, I've kissed Velt
        Radzika, my bed is taken, my things are packed, the taxi is due an
        moment.

He   Damn it! Why this urgency to get back to Moscow?

She   I have to go there as soon as possible. My husband will be there ir
        the next few days. He wants to see me, he's very much looking
        forward to it.

He   He isn't.

She   I say he is.

He   You're telling lies! He isn't looking forward to it at all.

She   (with a sharp change) Perhaps I am telling lies. What's to be done
        What's to be done?

He   Yes, what, indeed? (Pause) Don't be upset. I'm being impossible
        I've simply let myself go—yes, I have.

She   Yes, yes, it's all catastrophic.

He   Catastrophic?

She   Of course! The zip on my suitcase is broken and half my things are
        hanging out.

He   Yes, that is bad. But it can be mended.

She   I must have been very nervous when I was packing. I shouldn't have
        been so fierce with it! (Claps her hands) Oh God, I've had an awfu
        day.

He   (gloomy) Me too. I had a letter from my daughter. You know, I was
        so looking forward to seeing her.

She   And now . . . ?

He   She is not coming.

She   An accident?

He   No, not really. From a sane point of view, it's nothing.

She   But still?

He   You see . . . Well, I told you, my daughter and her husband live in
        Japan. He's a very nice man. He used to go in for sport. He's calmed
        down quite a bit lately. And she spends her leave with me, every
        year. Only last year she couldn't come. He just had to go and see his

aunt in Georgia. Well, she couldn't make it. I had such hopes for this autumn, but now it's fallen through again. They're going to Samarkand. It seems he's never been there. And on their way back they have business in Moscow and she doubts if she'll get here. It's a pity, of course . . . I've been very busy getting, everything ready— laid in drinks, all sorts of sweets. And I bought a new divan, terribly unusual the way it's made. Yes, pity. She says next summer without fail.

She	*(quietly)* Damn!
He	What was that for?
She	Oh, nothing.

Long pause.

He	I suppose so.
She	What was that for?
He	Nothing either.
She	The taxi!
He	Yes, it's here.
She	It's stopped by the sign. I'll go and tell him to come right up.
He	*(without a shout)* Just a moment!
She	What?
He	*(hastily)* I wanted to say . . . I've got an idea, a very sound idea. My daughter's room is absolutely empty. And I got it all ready, you know. The windows face the sea and you could spend a whole week there. I shan't bother you, I assure you. You don't have to see me at all, if you'd rather not. On the other hand, why shouldn't we have tea and jam together in the evening?
She	I'm very sorry, but believe me, it's quite impossible.
He	Why ever not?
She	No, no . . . Never. *(She runs out towards the waiting taxi)*

SCENE FIVE

Her thirty-first day.

At Rodion Nikolayevich's country house the table has been laid with a festive touch. Lidya Vasilyevna and Rodion Nikolayevich are wandering about.

The sun has not quite set. The sky is clear; it is a quiet, cool day towards the end of August.

She	What are you looking for?
He	We've done a splendid job this week and moved everything around.

It feels more snug of course but I'm not used to it. And I just can't find my blue shirt.

She   Don't be angry, I washed it yesterday and put it away in the little cupboard.

He   That was a mistake. I wash my own shirts. It gives me confidence and cheers me up.

She   Sewing buttons on your shirts and jackets is not exactly a hobby of yours.

He   I take my time over it, that's all. But in the last few days all my buttons have somehow sewn themselves on.

She   Sorry, I confess that for nearly forty years I've been tireless in sewing buttons on all kinds of jackets.

He   I am proud my jacket finds itself in such varied and distinguished company.

She   When you're angry, you lose all your charm.

He   There are a lot of things I don't like.

She   For instance?

He   I don't know. *(Looks at his watch)* Come on, it's late. Time for supper.

They fuss round the table.

May I propose a toast?

She   You may.

He   *(raises his glass to her)* Thank you.

She   Is that all?

He   I will repeat the toast. *(Full of feeling)* Thank you.

She   That's much better.

He   I always prefer a short toast.

She   Quite right. Why drag it out when the glasses are full.

He   We agree. Remarkable!

They sit down.

She   I must say this cheese you bought is a great success. Much better than the one I bought the day before yesterday.

He   But what about your liver sausage! Mine is very inferior.

She   I wouldn't say that. Your smoked eel looks delicious. I'm so glad you're wearing that astonishingly beautiful tie.

He   Yes, it's astonishingly fashionable too. And it's all of thirty years old.

She   *(pours out the wine)* Your tie, well done! What else shall we drink to?

He   I've expressed all my thoughts. It's your turn now.

She   *(raises her glass)* To the month of August. And to you, to a certain extent. You appeared in August. With the rain, the sunrise, the corner patisserie and old Riga. I lived without knowing any of it. And suddenly it all appeared. Not in my sleep for once—that's the funny part. For me this August is a kind of summing-up . . . of everything. A special benefit, as you might say. To the participants. To August!

>*They drink.*

(quietly) Are you disappointed?

He   *(very quietly)* Why?

She   I just chatter on.

He   *(slight pause)* You're wonderful.

She   Oh, no . . . Stop.

He   All right. Stop. *(Pause)* Actually, why stop?

She   You know as well as I do.

He   I don't know.

She   *(pause)* I'm very fond of flowers, the flowers that even today you left at the cemetery.

He   They will always be there. Nothing can change that.

She   Quite right.

He   *(pause)* It's been a good week.

She   Very good.

He   Why are you smiling?

She   I've just been working out our combined ages.

He   Oh, that's really funny.

She   But it was a good week.

He   Very.

She   It's the right moment to go away. *(Looks at her watch)*

He   Is the taxi late?

She   Not yet.

He   It will come.

She   Of course. *(Pours out the wine)* And the last toast . . . to going away!

>*They drink.*

Well, I think that's that.

He   Yes, that's it.

She   I'm afraid.

He   Why?

She   *(points to her suitcase)* My poor zip.

He   I've mended it.

She   Yes, of course, that's fine. *(With enthusiasm)* Well, I'll get on the train—and that will be that. I'll be off. I love travelling!

He   It's good to travel.

She   You feel free. You go where you like!

He   Yes, that's right.

She   You don't depend on anyone. Well, isn't it wonderful?

He   Marvellous !

She   After all, someone on their own ... He ... She ... *(With a strange gesture)* Hm ? True, isn't it ?

He   *(enthusiastic)* Yes, indeed !

She   You're your own master and free ! Completely free.

He   Absolutely ! Wonderful, isn't it ?

                        Taxi hoots.

She   Taxi.

He   Yes. It's here.

She   Thank God. *(Pause)* At last.

He   Yes, that's it—off you go then.

She   *(in a sudden rush)* When you're in Moscow, you will phone me, won't you ?

He   Of course I will. Thank you.

She   And I thank you. It was all very funny.

He   We're sure to see each other again.

She   Oh yes, we'll keep in touch.

He   Take care of yourself.

She   Good-bye. *(Crying out, genuinely frightened)* Oh, don't carry my cases, they're much too heavy. It's bad for you.

He   Nonsense ! They aren't heavy. I'll give them to the driver. I shan't be a moment. *(He goes out with the cases)*

                        She takes a picture-frame from one of her bags, inserts a photograph of a woman from the side-table. He returns.

        That's it. Everything on board.

She   It's a hobby of mine. I make frames. I make them for all my friends. I've made one for you. In my spare time. Otherwise your photograph will stand there collecting dust. It's untidy. Especially for someone in the forces. Thank you again. No, no, don't see me off.

                        She runs out.

                        He goes to the picture in the frame, then returns to the table, pours himself a glass of wine, looks at it but does not drink it. Aimlessly he wanders round the room, then urgently runs to the door, stops, takes his heart in his hands, smiles ironically and goes to the armchair. He sits down quietly. He closes his eyes and looks as though he has sat down for ever. Music starts up quietly; it is her song of the circus.

        "The circus tent is wide and high,
        To hold our glitter and our daring,
        The big parade of talent passes by
        The acrobats, the band with music blaring !

But you'll forget those pleasant times we met;
The artiste's voice, her eyes, the song she sang you.
The parts she played—yes, all will quickly fade.
Except her lingering memories of you.

While we are here and we exist,
We are the wonder of the circus.
While we remain, we'll always be the same:
The wonder and the magic of the circus."

She reappears.

I couldn't go . . . It's awful . . . I sent the taxi away.

He   *(quietly)* Thank you.

She   I don't know what to say.

He   Don't say anything. *(Pause; he smiles)* You know, I almost died.

She   Yes . . . Funny . . . I suppose all my life I've been coming to meet you.

Curtain.

www.ingramcontent.com/pod-product-compliance
Lightning Source LLC
LaVergne TN
LVHW051807080426
835511LV00019B/3433